"DEAR WITBONES"

Ask A Humorist!

Agony Uncle Advice for the Laughlorn

B. ELWIN SHERMAN
Curry Burn Press ψ New Hampshire

BOOKS BY B. ELWIN SHERMAN

The Miradors – Descensions of A Man

George W. Bush – On The Trips of His Tongue – A Linguistic Legacy

HumorUs (With the NetWits)

Toolkit In Paradise – The Self-Helpless Guide To A Decade of American Wit & Wisdom

Caught In The Shower Without A Pencil

Opening Closures – A Young Mother's Dying Declarations

Walk Tall and Carry A Big Watering Can

In Watermelon Salt – The Lost Richard Brautigan

© 2017 by B. Elwin Sherman

All rights reserved. No part of this book may be reproduced, stored in a retrieval system or transmitted in any form or by any means without the prior written permission of the author, except by a reviewer who may quote brief passages in a review for print media or internet newspapers, magazines or journals.

ISBN-13: 978-0-9982494-0-7

Designed & composed in Cambria Regular
at Curry Burn Press

Cover Art design by B. Elwin Sherman
Caricatures by Mike Marland
Research and connubial Attaboys by Diane Sherman

Printed in the U.S.A.

Published by:
Curry Burn Press, P.O. Box 300, Bethlehem, NH 03574
www.dearwitbones.com

"I've had a call to literature of a low order, i.e. Humorist. It is nothing to be proud of, but it is my strongest suit."

--- Samuel Langhorne Clemens

DEDICATION:

For Diane

and all those at their wit's end on the starting lines.

"DEAR WITBONES"

Table of Discontents

Sun Believer in Bangor   11
Fish Story in Franconia   13
Lonely in Littleton   15
Witless in Wells River   16
Hunkered Down in Haverhill   17
Cash Poor in Cornish   18
Swamped in Saratoga   19
No In-Law in Lockhart   22
House Divided in Houston   24
Agonizing in Akron   26
Coin Toss in Thomasville   28
Wishy-Washy in Waco   30
Land of the Lost in Lincoln   31
Ready to Roll in Rumney   32
Hoggin' It in Hermosa Beach   33
Not Smiling in Saginaw   37
Humorless in Hudson   38
Barking in Bethlehem   41
Defrosting in Dalton   42
Buck Fever in Barlow   43
Cat Chow in Chelmsford   45
Odd Man Out in Orford   46
Rocket Sled in Ryegate   48
Not a Dentist in Dayton   50
Headache in Hillsborough   52
Pickle in Palm Beach   54

Still Alive and Well in West Haven   55
Saturated in Spavinaw   57
Out of Goobers in Grants Pass   59
Upset Abutter in Bristol   61
Hobson's Choice in Hickory   63
Juicy Memorabilia in Madison   65
Bottom's Up in Boston   66
Held Up in Hendersonville   68
No News in Northfield   70
Perplexed in Peacham   71
Bigger in Barrington   73
Not a Wild Woman in Webster   75
Woman Wondering Where in Washington, D.C.   79
Student Whisperer in Waltham   83
No Appetite in New Orleans   86
Nom de Groom in Grafton   88
Not Dumb or Deaf in Danville   91
Finger Foods in Freeport   94
Dog-Dazed in Darien   96
Leaning in Lake Charles   98
Corpulent Calico Kitty in Cloverdale   99
Freaked Out in Flagler Beach   100
Looking Back in Lewisburg   101
Bare in Santa Barbara   102
Confused in Corpus Christi   104
Sexless in Swansboro   107

INTRODUCTION

witboner

[whit-bon-er]

Word Origin: noun

1. A question submitted to B. Elwin Sherman's agony uncle advice column.
2. Any individual who poses such a question.

Trouble on the homefront? Overworked at the office? Pets too picky? Can't find the humor in anything anymore? DEAR WITBONES may just change your life, with a smile or two to spare.

One disclaimer: If you need serious lovelorn help from an "agony aunt," please call your mother's sister first. If she's busy and already has enough trouble with your agony uncle, DEAR WITBONES is here for you.

You could do a lot worse, and if you're here, you probably have.

Thanks for WITBONING, and please keep me posted.

B.E.S.

DEAR WITBONES:

"I saw a story about a guy in North Carolina who is worried about solar panels installed in his town 'sucking all the energy out of the sun.' I laughed at first, but then I thought about it a while. I know that you're no scientist, and it's clear that I'm not one either, but is there ANY reason to fear that we could go too far with solar power? --- SUN BELIEVER IN BANGOR

Dear SUN BELIEVER: As an energy-seeking species, we went through something similar a few decades ago, when people worried that if we built too many tidal power stations, the resulting water friction would slow down the earth's rotation.

I'm married to a scientist, and she informs me that yes, in fact, harnessing the power of the ocean does put the brakes on our big blue marble, but the effect is so negligible that we'll be okay for the next few hundred million years or so. She explains this by telling me all about "angular momentum" and "rotational kinetic energy."

Yowza! I don't know why I find it so sexy, but it's always a turn-on when she talks science-y to me. Sometimes I'll ask her things like why we all don't have identical fingerprints or why no two snowflakes are exactly alike, just to hear her whisper sweet somethings like "volar pad regressions" and "deuterium atoms". That kind of pillow talk keeps the spice in our love life.

I did ask her about your life-sucking sun anxiety, and she told me to assure you that you needn't worry. We can't deplete the sun's energy simply by redirecting it after it gets here. She then went on talking "parabolic troughs" and "heliostat power towers" and I'm now ready to jump her bones.

Thanks for WITBONING, and please keep me posted.

DEAR WITBONES:

"I had to bring home tuna fish for my cat when the store ran out of her favorite kitty chow. Now, she'll only eat tuna fish. How can I get her back on track?" --- FISH STORY IN FRANCONIA

Dear FISH STORY: It's well-known that cats have the ability to see ghosts. They can also levitate rapidly without any apparent means of (forgive me) catapulting themselves, and will often do this without warning or apparent provocation.

These two abilities suggest that cats have a deeper visual acuity than we can comprehend. As a dog-person living with two cats, I think I can help. You have two options:

1. Feed your cat tuna fish. An expensive route, but tuna fish is chockfull of Omega-3 fatty acids, and research shows that these polyunsaturates may be helpful in treating anxiety and depression.

We know that cats are the only creatures that can simultaneously appear nervous and gloomy while defying gravity, so this may be beneficial. It may not be, however. The university researchers who discovered this are the same ones who determined, after lengthy field tests and time trials, that as joggers get older, they don't run as fast.

2. Try some deception. Save the tuna fish can labels, carefully remove them, and place them on cat food cans. DO NOT let your cat see you doing this

unless you want your ankle used as a permanent scratching post.

Thanks for WITBONING, and please keep me posted.

DEAR WITBONES:

"I'm tired of looking for love in all the wrong places, and still no Mr. Right in sight. My friends keep telling me to go online, so I want to get a computer. Then what?" --- LONELY IN LITTLETON

Dear LONELY: There are no "wrong places" to look for love. It's just as possible, these days, to make the wrong choices in the right places, so first of all, don't rule out anything, or anywhere.

Mr. Right could be sweeping up in the pool hall, and Mr. Wrong might be curating at the art museum. Keep your options open.

As for a new computer, it sounds like this is your first outing with one, an impressive standalone feat. I don't know how you've managed to get this far in life living only in physical space. Are you human?

If you answered yes, you'll probably have better luck seducing the guy at the computer store than you will making your way through a Windows learning curve and diving into the cyber singles circuit.

Or, next time, try passing up the Byzantine Art exhibition, and instead drop in for a game of eight-ball on the way home.

Thanks for WITBONING, and please keep me posted.

DEAR WITBONES:

"My kids are all grown up but they won't leave home. I thought these would be my Golden Years but I'm still shelling out money for gas, buying milk by the barrel, and I can't find my phones or remote control. What can I do?" --- **WITLESS IN WELLS RIVER**

Dear WITLESS: If you're in your "Golden Years," then your kids must still be living at home in their fifties. I'm not surprised that you've finally lost your "remote control," because that's obviously the only kind of control you've had for some time.

If your middle-aged offspring haven't gotten the hint by now, they never will. At this late date, the only way left for you to change their lives is by changing yours. I'd suggest the following:

Stop buying groceries and remove your car battery. Then, start a naked tuba & bagpipes band and have nightly rehearsals at your house.

Fake a few heart attacks.

Start talking to dead people at supper.

When you write-in six months from now complaining that you never see your children anymore, we'll deal with it.

Thanks for WITBONING, and please keep me posted.

DEAR WITBONES:

"The days will soon be getting longer, but not fast enough for me. I've thought of going to Florida but I'm afraid of manatees. How can I last until spring?" --- **HUNKERED DOWN IN HAVERHILL**

DEAR HUNKERED DOWN: I don't want to alarm you, and try not to think about this, but manatees have been spotted as far north as Cape Cod. This means that if one of them turned left into Connecticut and followed the river, with a portage or two it could eventually make its way into Haverhill, NH, coming ashore at Bedell Bridge State Park, and with the help of a sympathetic local motorist, arrive at your house.

If you hear a heavy thudding sound on your porch, I wouldn't answer the door.

Meanwhile, try a sun lamp.

Thanks for WITBONING, and please keep me posted.

DEAR WITBONES:

"Help! I have a lot of unpaid bills and the bill collectors are getting sick of my same old excuses. These people don't seem to have any sense of humor at all, but I thought maybe you could come up with something I could try." --- CASH POOR IN CORNISH

Dear CASH POOR: I feel your pain, and as a humorist with unpaid bills (are there any other kind?), my experience with humorless bill collectors prompts me to suggest the following. It's a method that has always worked for me:

Write to all your creditors and ask if they've heard the one about the priest, the rabbi and the minister who walk into a bar, and the bartender says: "Hey! What is this? Some kind of joke?"

Oh, and don't forget to send them the money.

Thanks for WITBONING, and please keep me posted.

DEAR WITBONES:

"I'm being overrun by the clutter in my house. I try to throw out things but when I do, I just later replace them with even more stuff. My floors are piled high, and there are only narrow walkways left to get between rooms. I'm afraid I'll be discovered crushed by an avalanche of my own junk, but there's just too much for me to deal with now and I don't even know where to begin. Help! How can I stop making mountains out of molehills?" --- SWAMPED IN SARATOGA

Dear SWAMPED: Sounds like you're a victim of HCS, or "Hoard & Clutter Syndrome," formerly known as the "Packrat Syndrome." It's a form of OCD (Obsessive-Compulsive Disorder) and its origins lie in what my dad used to call, the "When I Was Your Age We'd Walk A Mile For A Dirt Sandwich And Be Glad To Get It" Syndrome.

I've checked, and there are 8,321 books on the subject, and that's just counting the "expert" guests on Dr. Phil and Oprah. If you're writing to me because you need some deep insights from an armchair psychologist, I can only tell you to not even THINK about reading these books. They won't help, and you have no more room.

The good news is, your question holds the key to solving this dilemma. No, you're not making mountains out of molehills, but you are trying to make molehills out of mountains. Fine if you're a mole, but you need the human version.

The solution is simple:

1. Empty your house of EVERYTHING. Yes, I said everything. Don't discriminate. You can't, anyway, not in your condition; that's why everything must go. Bag it, box it, throw it out the window, do whatever you have to do to get everything inside, outside. You're not attempting to determine what's trash and what's treasure. As I said, you're not capable of doing that, so don't try. You're a hoarder. Right now, you could find three good reasons for holding on to fuzzy green cheese or a broken right nostril inhaler.

So, for now, everything not nailed down? Out with it!

2. Done? Now, only bring back inside what you absolutely need to get through the day; let's say: a toothbrush, a box of Yodels, and bubble bath. Do this every day for a week, and no cheating. Lug only the essentials back into the house: mattress, soggy Twinkies (I know that if you had Yodels, you also had Twinkies), dirty towels, light bulbs, and your children.

3. If you haven't brought it back within a week, it's officially junk. Put out a "FREE STUFF" sign, and say the following out loud repeatedly until everything out there is gone: "I've never seen a hearse pulling a trailer." It's your new mantra. Eventually, all your cast-offs will disappear. Not to worry. Before it's over, someone will even take the sign. Free is free.

Now: how to keep from relapsing into your hoarding behavior?

Leave Florida and move up here to New Hampshire. We don't hoard.

We just hold onto things for the great-grandchildren.

Thanks for WITBONING, and please keep me posted.

DEAR WITBONES:

"My mother-in-law keeps telling my husband what a bad cook I am. I like to make healthy food and sometimes the tofu is rubbery, but as far as I can tell, there's nothing in HER kitchen except Hamburger Helper. How can I get her to butt out?" -- NO IN-LAW IN LOCKHART

Dear NO IN-LAW: Trust me, you don't WANT your mother-in-law to butt out, unless you're prepared to start mothering your mate.

First of all, tell him this joke:

Question: How does a mother-in-law screw in a light bulb?   Answer: She holds the bulb, stands still, and waits for the world to revolve around her.

With that in mind, and after the two-day argument that will follow, calm down and try looking at this from her point of view. When that fails (and I hate to say this, because I'm convinced that tofu IS rubber), don't fault yourself because of your inability to take the bounce out of curdled soybean milk. I'm told there actually is a product called Tofu Helper, but for my money, you could wrap it in bacon and vulcanize the stuff under the broiler and it wouldn't help.

If I might paraphrase: "The way to a man's stomach is through his mother's heart." Ask mom for her favorite Hamburger Helper recipes, moosh the tofu into the mashed potatoes (trust me, he won't know the difference) and don't have her over for dinner.

Thanks for WITBONING, and please keep me posted.

DEAR WITBONES:

"My husband is a Democrat and I'm a Republican. This has created a lot of tension in this house, and we're hardly speaking to each other. We're also now riding in separate cars, watching television in opposite ends of the house, eating dinner alone and, worst of all, no more lovemaking! How can I get him back in our bed and end this bickering?" --- HOUSE DIVIDED IN HOUSTON

Dear HOUSE DIVIDED: When any family dispute prompts you to retreat to an Abraham Lincoln speech, it's time for a radical intervention, and asking a humorist for advice does indeed show how desperate you are.

I may be paraphrasing, but when Lincoln said "The day will come when a house divided against itself will need at least two cars and two televisions," he knew where the American family (and the need for two bathrooms) was headed.

Your political party household dilemma might best be resolved by heralding another quote from Honest Abe. He once said: "If this is coffee, please bring me some tea; but if this is tea, please bring me some coffee."

This is not only the cause of friction in your home, but is also the same difference between your candidates, and you might try applying a tactic that will at least temporarily disarm both of you.

I'd suggest soft lighting, smooth music, spiked punch, sexy lingerie and the Libertarian Party.

Thanks for WITBONING, and please keep me posted.

DEAR WITBONES:

"Our college-attending daughters recently came home for summer break, and when they learned that we'd switched our political party status (I'd rather not say from what to what). They flipped out, and it's been non-stop criticism and sarcasm since. We're getting pretty sick of it, and aren't sure if we can hold out until they go back to school. Suggestions?" --- AGONIZING IN AKRON

Dear AGONIZING: You should first count yourself lucky that your daughters have only come home to visit. The cost of sending them to college is nothing compared to what you'd otherwise be shelling out for their upkeep under your roof. Count your blessings, and hide your munchies and cell phones.

Next, you must know that "flipped out" is the normal mindset for anyone attending college. I don't even remember the first six months of my enlistment in advanced academia, except to say that I've now traded-in flashbacks for flash forwards. Your daughters' newfound passions for politics will settle down and find their own ways.

You might be more concerned about how you will handle your suppressed hysteria on the day daughter number one appears at your door with what looks like the reincarnation of Sid Vicious, and you're seized with the prospect of having a tattooed blue-haired grandchild named "Ozone Peach."

Or, when daughter number two announces that she's found the true meaning of life in a religion that requires cave-dwelling.

Thanks for WITBONING, and please keep me posted.

DEAR WITBONES:

"I'm an African-American woman, and I feel like I'm always reduced to choosing between my heritage and my sex in everything I do. How did it come to this?" --- *COIN TOSS IN THOMASVILLE*

Dear COIN: This is a tough one. I've never been an African American or a woman, so I wouldn't presume to know the depths of your scope & practice of either. But, where I come from, your sex IS your heritage.

I hail from a long line of garbage taker-outers, for example. My grandfather was a lifelong GT-O, as was my father before me, for no reason I know other than they were men, I'm a man, and this is what we-men are expected to do.

Somewhere in that descendancy, we also became official domestic oil-changers and weed-whackers, but I think we were complicit in that. Yard work and the garage are great getaways from the stressors of marital bliss.

I once tried to help out around the house when my wife was ill. I did the laundry and washed the dishes. I meant well, of course, but after I put wool sweaters in the dryer and chipped the good china, I was quickly reassigned to my inherited and acquired duties/legacies.

Now, how does this translate into which way you should think and act? I'm sticking with my rewrite of Robert Frost's "The Road Not Taken":

*Two roads diverged in a wood, and I---
I took the other one.*

Thanks for WITBONING, and please keep me posted.

DEAR WITBONES:

"After twenty years of marriage, I know it sounds impossible at this late date, but I still can't decide if I'm a boxers or briefs kind of guy. My wife's no help, because she won't go near my underwear, either way. I'm baffled that I'm so baffled by this, because I've always not been an indecisive person. Suggestions?" --- WISHY-WASHY IN WACO

Dear WISHY-WASHY: Following along your own lines, it's often been said (by me) that Harry Truman wasn't the President who didn't decide not to drop the bomb. It doesn't seem to me that you're not facing a dissimilar pickle.

If I weren't you, I couldn't be any less cavalier, not about which skivvy you shouldn't choose to not wear, but which one you don't think wouldn't best undo the job when the wrong time didn't come.

I also wouldn't, if I weren't me, not stop reading Lewis Carroll to relax. Or not.

No thanks for not WITBONING, and please never try to not keep me unposted.

DEAR WITBONES:

"Why do 'city people' move to the country for the views and the trees, and the first thing they do is cut down the trees, put up fences with 'No Trespassing' signs, and build oversized houses that obstruct the views? Why don't they just stay where they are, and stop wrecking the country for us country folks?" --- LAND OF THE LOST IN LINCOLN

Dear LAND: Ah, you've hit a nerve that sends the ruralites among us (your host included) into near apoplexy, even though apoplexy is caused by a lack of oxygen, not frayed nerves. But, let's not quibble over precisely how or why we're made stupefied. I need to help you before you pass out.

There isn't much we can do about those folks "from away" who are urbanizing our home fronts. I'd suggest taking refuge in one of my favorite retreats: Ogden Nash.

City people are querulous and queasy,
And they'd rather die than not live easy.
And if they did die, they'd find fault
If they weren't put in an air-conditioned vault.

Thanks for WITBONING, and please keep me posted.

(Columnist note: The following two Witboners need to hook up and ride.)

DEAR WITBONES:

"I have a problem! I keep having these dreams that I am on my old motorcycle heading through the mountains. Problem is, while I am dreaming, my partner tells me I am actually trying to kick-start my bike in bed, and she keeps waking up with leg bruises. What should I do? Risk that I'll keep kicking her in my sleep or buy a newer bike with an electric start? Help me, dude! It's getting near time to ride!" --- READY TO ROLL IN RUMNEY

Dear READY: As a fellow motorcycle owner, I've been right where you are with the same problem, but with a slightly different twist. I do have an electric start, and in my sleep I'm always grabbing my partner's wrist and pressing it with my thumb. And, because I also have highway bars with elevated foot rests, she awakens to the wrist pinch and the sight of me lifting my feet in the air.

Trust me; this sends an entirely different message, and one that I highly recommend.

Time to upgrade and enjoy the ride, dude.

Thanks for WITBONING, and please keep me posted.

DEAR WITBONES:

"I have a sex question, and please don't think I'm crazy: My wife and I have an active sex life, and we love to experiment with different ways and places to get it on. Today, she suggested having sex on our Harley-Davidson. I like the idea, but I'm worried that we could crack up (and it's a new bike!). Any helpful hints on how to keep it safe without giving up the thrills?" --- *HOGGIN' IT IN HERMOSA BEACH*

Dear HOGGIN' IT': To avoid serious injury and/or divorce, your question deserves some extra room, so I'm expanding this week's space just for you. You wouldn't be the first couple to do the deed on a motorcycle, but if you're not careful, you could be the last (in your lives, anyway).

Yes, there certainly are a few cautions to consider:

First, congrats on the new bike! I'd start out with the breaking-in advice my Harley dealer gave me when we got our new Road King: "Baby it for the first 600 miles, then ride it like you stole it."

Same principle applies here, and I'd begin as you would normally in foreplay with only some soft kissing (no tongues just yet) and light upper body caresses with the bike on the kickstand. Wear all your leathers. Engine can be on or off, but if it's on, that will limit you, time-wise. It's okay for YOU to overheat, but not your air-cooled engine! Either way, your hog should be stationary and both of you must remain in traditional riding postures during these initial phases of lovemaking.

If you want to preface this activity with a visit to a biker bar, a day-long ride with your H.O.G. buddies, or a shopping spree in your Harley-Davidson dealer's clothes & accessories department, it will only serve to later heighten your pleasure.

From there, work your way into short jaunts around town (out of town would be better. WAY out.). Now, you must master what sex therapists call "the art of distraction," i.e. how to keep your bodies always in synch with the machine. Erotic pleasures can rapidly evaporate when you suddenly encounter an off-road stationary object. You might find that it didn't lessen your libido, but, trust me; your wife will never ride with you again.

Take your stimulating cues from Harley's new six-speed transmissions. This gives you an extra level of arousal, and an opportunity to include another plateau of delight.

For example, you can add heavy petting to light smacking (tongues now allowed), or playful biting to firm nibbling, but don't lose sight of your RPM's. Also, if you just think of the mechanics of operating a motorcycle as a general guide to sensual techniques, you'll find yourselves naturally making the right moves: throttling-up, releasing, clutching, shifting, re-engaging – and all the while increasing your overall speed and distance as everything else passes by you, and you go faster and deeper into the ... countryside.

Don't forget the brakes! (See: objects, stationary). How you apply them, either front or rear, should be instinctive and in harmony with your environment. And, remember to always accelerate coming out of a curve.

Positions? Once you've reduced your outer garments to a maximum of chaps (clothes made specifically for what we'll call "ease of facilitation"), how you then set yourselves on your new hog is purely elective. You should, however, consider your body types, weight, height and breadth as they relate to your bike's frame and engine size. Use common sense, along with personal preferences. Don't try for the same high-end peak performance you'd get on a Sportster if you have a Fat Boy.

If you're blessed with an Electra-Glide ... well ... half your learning curve is already built-in.

Pay the same attention to your sexual bodies as you do to both the rules of the road and motorcycle operation, e.g. know and utilize your turning radiuses, adjustable seat heights, lean angles and best foot placements. It doesn't hurt to bone-up on lane changing, uphill shifting, regular maintenance, and operating on slippery surfaces.

Use SIPDE, the Motorcycle Safety Foundation's acronym for "Scan, Identify, Predict, Decide &

Execute," and apply it to your erogenous zones for a full and complete ride.

You might also adopt "NBD," the slang motorcycle acronym for "Never Been Dropped," as a personal credo when pursuing your new exhilarations. Remember: Good for your bike? Good for your partner (and vice-versa). Especially at high speeds.

Thanks for WITBONING, and please keep me posted.

DEAR WITBONES:

"I'm not anyone's perfect 10, so I'm hoping to find a guy who likes a 'good sense of humor'. The trouble is I'm also not very funny. Can you offer some tips on how to convince a man that I can be female and funny?" --- NOT SMILING IN SAGINAW

Dear HUMORLESS: A "Perfect 10" does not exist, so let's first rid you of that notion. Besides, one man's Perfect 10 is another man's lawn tractor, so just stop right there. Unless you can compete with John Deere's new four-wheel drive X729 on an emotional level, and you yourself "operate easily with a single dash-mounted switch," especially in the morning, you're going about this all wrong.

I'm going to leave you to prove to him that you're female, but you only need to convince him that he THINKS you're funny. For the male animal, this is the same thing, and you're already funnier than you think you are, or you wouldn't be seriously asking how to get a man to think like you want him to. To accomplish that, you need only meet two conditions:

1. One of you is a man.
2. You're both breathing.

So, just be yourself. For most of us, that's as funny as we need to be, intentional or not.

Thanks for WITBONING, and please keep me posted.

(Columnist note: Not long after the previous female funny Witboner arrived, this one came in from the opposite sex.)

Dear WITBONES:

"Due to circumstances beyond my control, I find myself divorced and alone in life, looking for a female partner. I've just read a woman's magazine article that listed the top five things a woman finds most attractive in a man, and number one was his ability to make her laugh. The trouble is that I don't know how to be funny. Can you offer some tips on how I can convince a woman that I have a great sense of humor?" --- **HUMORLESS IN HUDSON**

Dear HUMORLESS: I recently dealt with a woman with your same problem (let's hope she's reading this). You haven't given me much to go on. I don't know your occupation or religion, or lack of either, and you also didn't mention your age or political persuasion, all great launch pads for humor. These particulars would help me suggest how you can best find and express your inner funny.

I could better direct you if I knew you were a Baptist or a sun worshipper or a retired ombudsman, but I'll just go with a one-size-should-fit-all.

We'll just assume, for starters, that when you cite "circumstances beyond my control" as the reason for your single-status, you're not referring to your picture appearing on the post office bulletin board, or that you've been the object of a recent international in-flight quarantine. Most everything else can be tweaked as you go.

It's a well-known fact that women love to laugh, because the act of laughing prompts a biochemical reaction in women which affects a part of their brain that regulates erotic thoughts and impulses. This is why female actors are always seen suppressing their laughter in Viagra commercials.

That same part of the brain, in men, dictates why we don't care if our socks match.

Now, if you want to give your new potential gal the giggles, you must first disabuse yourself of your humorless self-assessment. Of course you're funny. You've been through a divorce, which means you've seen the depths of despair --- the place where hilarity lives like a troll under a bridge --- and survived.

I'll offer just one general "tip" on how to be funny the next time you find yourself attempting to impress a woman with your wit:

Every man is funny. Just look at how we're built. You're reading women's magazines looking for ways to attract a woman? I suggest that you instead rehearse cracking yourself up. Because of your grim self-evaluation, it would be best to do this naked, in front of a mirror, with props. Later, when you confess to your date that you did this to impress her, she will never take you seriously again.

Thanks for WITBONING, and please keep me posted.

DEAR WITBONES:

"My neighbor's dog won't stop barking. I've tried everything I can think of from calling the Animal Control guy to earplugs but nothing seems to work for long. The dog's owners are gone all day and don't have to listen to him, but he barks constantly even when they're home. My husband isn't bothered by it at all, but I can't stand it another day. What can I do?" --- BARKING IN BETHLEHEM

Dear BARKING: No dog barks for no reason, so there's a good place to start.

In her book "NO BAD DOGS," the late Barbara Woodhouse points out that there are no difficult dogs, only difficult dog owners. So, in reality, it's your neighbor, not his dog, barking at you. Think of it this way, and you'll soon realize what it is you're doing that's making him bark. Now, stop doing this, and instead do whatever you need to do to make him whimper and fall silent.

Just apply the same training that apparently worked on your husband.

Thanks for WITBONING, and please keep me posted.

DEAR WITBONES:

"I know it's not politically correct and I feel guilty about saying it, but with another New Hampshire winter upon us, I'm looking forward to global warming. A friend says that I don't know the difference between climate and weather. I say they're the same thing. Am I wrong? --- DEFROSTING IN DALTON

Dear DEFROSTING:
Here's a simple test: Have you ever asked anyone with a hangover if they're feeling "under the climate"?

I see that you're finding it hard to reconcile the difference, especially when The Farmer's Almanac says that we're in for a record-setting cold winter, but you must try to apply the same "you can't get there from here" logic that we're so fond of here. Or, there, if you can make it.

If you're guilt-struck because you find the notion of retreating glaciers, rising oceans, ozone depletion and species extinction preferable to a couple extra weeks of shoveling snow, perhaps you have a problem with what psychiatrists like to call "sanity."

I suggest you bundle up and stop reading advice columns from humorists.

Thanks for WITBONING, and please keep me posted.

DEAR WITBONES:

"My savings account is being charged five bucks a month for a 'maintenance' fee because it is 'dormant.' If I occasionally withdraw money, they don't charge the fee, but if I continue to just save money, and I live long enough, they will take it all because I tried to save it. Should I just bury my money in the back yard, or stuff it in my mattress?"
--- BUCK FEVER IN BARLOW

Dear BUCK FEVER: When it comes to domestic money matters, most people turn to Suze Orman, the "internationally acclaimed personal finance expert." For my money, I like a continental flair in my personal finance expert. I may not know what the Belarusian ruble is doing, but if it means I'm paying more for Yoo-Hoo, I want my PFE to know.

And, I like Suze. Right away, you can tell she has savings savvy by how she divested herself of the letter "s," dropped the letter "i," invested a "z," and still socked away enough to keep two syllables in her first name for her retirement. Plus, she makes piles of money selling books on how to make money. Smart cookie.

But, your question has me wondering: wouldn't you rather learn how to get a better bang for your buck by reading an author who has made and squandered a dozen fortunes, spends all her royalties at the track, and now lives in her car? Wouldn't you learn more from someone who's worked her way *down* the ladder of success?

As for your bank, of course it penalizes you for saving. Any institution that imposes a fine when you bounce a check, hitting you up for hefty fees when you're obviously broke, is operating normally. My advice?

Bury your mattress in your back yard. Just don't be foolish enough to put your money in it.

Thanks for WITBONING, and please keep me posted.

DEAR WITBONES:

"My cat doesn't seem to like me that much. He comes around at feeding time, snuggles up and purrs, but then he suddenly just disappears. Actually, I'm having the same problem with my boyfriend, if you know what I mean. Do you have any suggestions?" --- *CAT CHOW IN CHELMSFORD*

Dear CAT CHOW: Unusual that your boyfriend is acting like your cat. Typically, boyfriends mimic dog behavior, i.e. relieving themselves on your front lawn, fetching everything back into the house that you throw away, and rolling over on command. So, when a boyfriend adopts the same eat 'n run aloofness more common to felines, something else is wrong. Somewhere, you've been remiss in training him properly.

I would start first by changing the quality, quantity and frequency of your "feeding time," (if you know what I mean) and keep the treats to a teasing minimum.

Nature loves a miser. Your boyfriend will follow suit and come back wanting.

Thanks for WITBONING, and please keep me posted.

DEAR WITBONES:

"I know this sounds silly, but that's why I'm writing to you. Dr. Phil would probably tell me that I have an obsessive something or other. My problem is that I have to have things come out even: laundry, meals, checking account, even filling my car with gas. Everything needs to be an even number, or I feel like I'm out of whack. As you noticed, I'm sending you two copies of this letter! It's now getting me into trouble at work, where I have to generate customer invoices. So far, I've blamed the duplicates on a computer glitch, but I think my boss isn't buying it." --- ODD MAN OUT IN ORFORD

Dear ODD MAN ODD MAN: Yes yes I I can can help help.

First, Dr. Phil would be right; you've got a good neurosis going on there, but he's on channel 13. Odd number. That's no good for you, and try not to think about it. At least try not to think twice about it.

Also, it's unclear whether you're obsessed with even numbers, or have a fear of odd ones, or both. No matter. Obsession or phobia, the net effect of either is the same for both, so that should put you at ease. Two for one and all for two, either way.

You must learn to make friends with the oddities in your life. Dr. Phil would call this "habituating," which you'll notice has 11 letters. But, relax! Add 11 letters to 13 channels and you get a safe, friendly, 24. Whew!

Now, get a second job. You'll find your comfort zone in two jobs, two bosses, two desks, two computers and two office parties. I'm sorry it took me five paragraphs to tell you this.

Thanks for WITBONING (nine letters. Again, I apologize, but at least I'm sorry twice), and please keep me posted at least once. The first time.

Thanks for WITBONING, and please keep me posted.

DEAR WITBONES:

"This may be outside your area of expertise, but I have a car problem. Whenever I accelerate rapidly, the car hesitates, almost like it's going to stall, then I hear a sound which I can only describe as a kind of 'kah-tickbang whooshy' noise. This repeats a few times, then the car takes off like I was shot out of a cannon. What gives?" --- ROCKET SLED IN RYEGATE

Dear ROCKET SLED: You didn't mention your automobile's year, make & model, but this is a common problem with any car made in the U.S.A. between 1902 and 2017.

We might first examine why you're finding it necessary to "accelerate rapidly." Unless you're robbing banks or are habitually late for dialysis, this is not a good practice. It greatly reduces gas mileage, and exponentially increases your need to decelerate rapidly, especially in moose country.

And, you're quite right about my lack of mechanical prowess. I'm most familiar with a "kah-tickbang whooshy" sound when I first get up in the morning and just make it to the bathroom in time. But, I do know that combustion engines best start and run smoothly by integrating the right amounts of gasoline, oil, prayer and cursing, depending on the weather, police cars and size of the moose.

And, try to remember that there are people in this world who do indeed make their livings being shot out of cannons. You might consider this.

Thanks for WITBONING, and please keep me posted.

DEAR WITBONES:

"Last month while brushing my upper denture, it slipped out of my hand and broke in two pieces. I put it back together with Duct Tape, but it only lasts for a week or two, and then I have to start all over. What else can I do?" --- NOT A DENTIST IN DAYTON

Dear NOT A DENTIST: First off, your letter is suspect because of what everyone knows as a universal truth: Duct Tape will permanently fix anything, broken or unbroken.

You may not know that Duct Tape saved the lives of the Apollo 13 astronauts. It was also used to firm-up a makeshift fender on a lunar rover. Duct Tape is, in fact, so revered by NASA that it is included in an operations manual as a means of dealing with an "acute psychosis emergency."

I wish I was kidding. When a space station inhabitant flips his/her wig, Duct Tape, in lieu of a weightless straightjacket, is our American space program's preferred restraint mechanism.

Now, aren't you embarrassed? If Duct Tape can quell a zero gravity Cuckoo's Nest uprising, it can certainly fix your faux choppers. You must be doing something wrong (applying it on only sticky-side up?), but that's beside the point.

Just because you CAN do something doesn't mean that you SHOULD. You should begin by having your spouse immediately restrain you (and now you know how) before transporting you to the dentist. No one who fixes their dentures with Duct Tape should be walking around loose.

Thanks for WITBONING, and please keep me posted.

DEAR WITBONES:

"My problem is my co-worker. She's a wonderful person and a good employee, but she has the most obnoxious laugh. Not only is it loud and cackly, but she adds this snorting sound that makes me shudder, and sometimes she just laughs for no apparent reason. I work in the cubicle next to hers and I'm not sure how much longer I can take it. Without hurting her feelings, how do I tell her that she's making me crazy?" --- HEADACHE IN HILLSBOROUGH

Dear HEADACHE: Whenever I need an explanation for a good laugh, I turn to science, and here I'll hold with neurobiologist Robert R. Provine's assertion that "laughter is not about humor; it is about relationships between people." He should know. He spent ten years researching "2000 cases of naturally occurring laughter." This is laughter not apparently provoked by anything funny. Personally, I think Laughing Bob missed his calling as a humor columnist.

Thus, according to Professor Provine, your co-worker is not laughing AT anyone, rather she's cackle-snorting because of her relationship, or lack of it, WITH someone (probably the person closest to her, cubicle-wise. Ahem.). I'd start there.

She is either seeking your attention or wants you to leave her alone. Her irritating, exaggerated hoots of laughter are compensatory mechanisms for either your advances or your lack of them. The less or more you ignore or rebuke her, the worse her hilarity outbreaks.

You need to stop doing, or not doing, whatever it is that's causing her to crack up "for no apparent reason." You could begin by wondering why you ever thought a humorist could help you with this. I'm still working on why I cry whenever I'm standing in line at the Department of Motor Vehicles.

Thanks for WITBONING, and please keep me posted.

DEAR WITBONES:

"Last night during supper I dropped a dill pickle on the floor. I brushed it off and ate it, thoroughly grossing out my college senior daughter who now thinks I'm disgusting. How can I convince her that what I did was not gross?" --- PICKLE IN PALM BEACH

Dear PICKLE: Once again, science has the answer. A Clemson University scientist has debunked the "five-second rule". This is the conventional wisdom that says if your pickle stays on the floor for less than five seconds, it's okay to eat. Foodologist Dr. Paul Dawson reports that "food dropped on surfaces contaminated with pathogens will pick up those bacteria immediately."

He and his team did extensive testing, dropping their pickles on various surfaces in timed intervals, discovering that wood or tile floors are much more infectious than carpets. I'm no rug bug scientist, but I'm calling this "the fuzzy factor."

But, I'm also certain that Dr. Dawson neglected to test the average sorority room floor, where six-month old Doritos under beds have been known to be consumed with no ill effects.

You may quote me the next time you dine with your daughter.

Thanks for WITBONING, and keep me posted.

DEAR WITBONES:

"I'm sick to death of being told how to live a long 'healthy' life. Drink coffee? Don't drink coffee. Alcohol is good? Alcohol is bad. Jog? Don't jog. Eat meat? Don't eat meat. Is there one wholesome longevity 'formula' that everyone can agree on?" --- **STILL ALIVE AND WELL IN WEST HAVEN**

Dear STILL ALIVE: Yes, there is one size in the human condition that fits all – one person at a time. I once asked a woman on the occasion of her hundredth birthday your very question, i.e. what a person should do to reach the century mark. Her answer was delightfully simple: "Don't die, you damn fool."

She went on to add how we should all learn to busy ourselves living with what we have, not dying from what we don't. "That's why God made hearing aids, eyeglasses, false teeth and scooters." For the record, she was a vegetarian and drank like a fish.

But, another gentleman who only passed away recently at the age of 112, was found to have long-subsisted on a diet of "sausages and waffles, with plenty of syrup." And, my own great-grandfather lived to the age of 101. He once said: "I smoked like a chimney, drank my own corn liquor, and philandered whenever I could." My grandfather, himself making it into his nonagenarian years, used to joke that his father's lifestyle "probably killed him just like that."

I knew yet another elder character who lived alone well into his nineties. He shunned human company, opting instead for a motley menagerie of cats and dogs, and for the last ten years of his life, he never washed. In fact, he dropped dead on the first day that visiting nurses gave him a sponge bath.

I'd suggest mixing and matching all of the above, until you find the life that suits you.

Meanwhile, "NEVER SWIM IN SHARK TANKS WITH A NOSEBLEED" might be the universal and uncontested longevity guarantee you're seeking. Otherwise, sorry, there is no one-size-fits-all rule for optimum health; give it up. Now, don't die, you damn fool, and eat what feels good.

Thanks for WITBONING, and please keep me posted.

DEAR WITBONES:

"My boyfriend thinks I'm too sensitive about this, but I can't look anywhere these days without seeing sex used as a way to sell everything. Sexy cars, sexy phones, even sexy gardening tools! What is this everywhere obsession we have with SEX?" --- SATURATED IN SPAVINAW

Dear SATURATED: Unless Google has a cyberjink in it, I only find one reference to "Spavinaw," and that's in Oklahoma: "the birthplace of Mickey Mantle." I don't see any connection between that and your feeling understated in an oversexed world, but DEAR WITBONES readers deserve an occasional celebrity fun fact with every column.

I also see that at your last census count there were "95.5 males for every 100 females" in Spavinaw. This means that somewhere in Spavinaw, there's half a man trying to juggle 1.045 girlfriends. This, too, probably doesn't directly relate to the burden you're feeling with libidinous pitchmen popping up everywhere, but perhaps we're getting close.

You must accept the notion that garden tools do indeed have a "sexy" clement to them. Personally, I've often felt sexy while weedwhacking, but I can't say the same for the reverse.

Also remember that you're looking at this from a woman's (I'm assuming) point of view, so I'm eliminating the math and substituting algebra, where X equals Y minus everything else.

If you're still only feeling 99.995 percent aroused, try looking at fewer advertisements and start tending your nasturtium bed bottomless. I'll wager that a greater consumer fraction of your boyfriend will appreciate it.

Thanks for WITBONING, and please keep me posted.

DEAR WITBONES:

"What is going on with Skippy Chunky Peanut Butter? Lately, I can only find it in small-size jars. Should I buy a case from my store, OR buy the bigger Creamy jars, spread Creamy on my bread and add chopped-up peanuts, OR complain to my grocer?" --- *OUT OF GOOBERS IN GRANTS PASS*

Dear OUT OF GOOBERS: Your letter is brand-specific. Let's start there.

I feel your pain, and I've checked Skippy's website. I couldn't find any detailed jar dimension information, but I did discover that a railroad boxcar holds 190,000 pounds of peanuts, or the equivalent of sixteen elephants. Do the math, and you'll find this also equals the heft of 1000 average-sized grocers. I can't imagine why a thousand grocers would all want to travel in one boxcar, but I like the visual.

Perhaps Skippy is part of a plot to unleash a New World Disorder by clouding our chunky childhood memories with this smaller, universal packaging. I remember peanut butter coming in five-gallon tubs. My mom kept them in the pantry with the milk pails of grape jelly.

Meanwhile, sure, if the purist in you can't stand it, add some diced peanuts to your Creamy. While you're at it, if you prefer a more dairy-oriented dip, you could pick the pecans out of your butter pecan ice cream. They only put them in there, anyway, because no one would buy "butter ice cream."

On second thought, this IS America. What was I thinking? I've Googled it and yes, there it is: butter ice cream. Deep-fried. On a stick. With jimmies. At the state fair. Sigh.

Thanks for WITBONING, and please keep me posted.

DEAR WITBONES:

"My problem is my neighbor. Practically overnight, he's become a slob. He's stopped cutting his grass, his garage is falling down, and his yard is full of junk cars. I try to keep my house, lawn and garden looking nice, and I know we're all entitled to live the way we want, but I'm afraid his messy property will now start to devalue mine. How can I get him to clean up his act?" --- UPSET ABUTTER IN BRISTOL

Dear UPSET: I once had your problem, but in reverse. Some time ago, my neighbor was always one-upping me: Whenever I'd cut my grass in the morning, he'd cut his later in the day, robbing me of ever having the shortest lawn. I tried timing it so I'd finish just as darkness set in, but his riding mower had headlights.

When I painted my house, he put on new cedar clapboards. When I had my gravel driveway re-graded, he paved his. When I reshingled my roof, he put in skylights. When I planted new bushes, he planted new trees. Last year, I decided that "keeping up with the Joneses" just wasn't important anymore.

When my two cars died, I parked them permanently out back. I now have handy resources when I need parts for my new clunker. When my garage started to fall in, I began thinking of it as rustic architecture. Somehow, the sight of my leaning garage makes me feel stronger. And, I've learned to love the wild, undulating look of an uncut lawn. Reminds me of my younger, carefree days.

If that makes you feel older and more troubled, I won't compete with you.

Thanks for WITBONING, and please keep me posted.

DEAR WITBONES:

"It looks like it's come down to choosing between wallpaper and paint. My daughter says wallpaper and my wife says paint, and they're both waiting for me to declare my preference. Can you see a way out of this no-win situation at home?" --- *HOBSON'S CHOICE IN HICKORY*

Dear HOBSON'S CHOICE: First, yours is not a true "Hobson's Choice," i.e. a situation where you must take what's offered to you or nothing at all. In your case, you have an alternative to nothing, which is one or the other. Your dilemma more resembles the figurative "Buridan's Ass," named after 14th Century French philosopher Jean Buridan. (This was 700 years ago, so we're talking donkey, not derrière.)

But, in that paradox, a donkey standing an equal distance between two piles of hay, starves to death when it can't decide which to eat. No good.

You might, however, really be facing a "Morton's Fork," named after a 15th Century English Lord Chancellor, John Morton. Here, you must choose between "two equally unpleasant alternatives." In your case, do you lie to your wife or your child? I'd suggest applying a "Sherman's Wangle":

Tell wife you're partial to paint and make her promise not to tell your daughter. Tell daughter you're on board with wallpaper, but not to let mom know. Neither will want to betray your trust or hurt the other's feelings, and you won't have to choose, not choose, or starve.

They're also both playing the "good Dad, bad husband" (and vice versa) card, and between the two of them, you're going to wind up with fake bricks, anyway.

Thanks for WITBONING, and please keep me posted.

DEAR WITBONES:

"I can't compete with people who find holy images in ordinary objects, but I did buy a quart of strawberries from a local farm, and I found one berry with a mooshed-in tip, and it's a ringer for Herbert Hoover. Should I try to sell this rarity on Ebay?" --- *JUICY MEMORABILIA IN MADISON*

Dear JUICY MEMORABILIA: No one will remember (but you can remind them in your Ebay listing) that Herbert Hoover once said: "A good many things go around in the dark besides Santa Claus." Your question leaves that assertion unchallenged.

Yes, certainly you should list your prized discovery on Ebay. As I write this, there is an "unused popsicle stick" posted for auction there. I wish I was kidding, but the current bid is $26.00. Another seller is about to make ten dollars on an "Empty pack of Kool-Aid." There are ten idiots out there bidding on these two items. In light of this, I've no doubt your Hoover-berry will knock the socks off the Presidential fruit memorabilia collectors.

Careful on the shipping, though. Unless you freeze, pack and send it properly, your winning bidder might end up receiving a likeness of a mooshed-in Woodrow Wilson. Much less collectible.

Thanks for WITBONING, and please keep me posted.

DEAR WITBONES:

"I've always wanted to hold a world record for something, but I'm no athlete. In fact, I'm female, small, and I'm all thumbs. But, when I see that a man is about to break the world record for sitting in over 90,000 seats in the Rose Bowl, I think, WOW, I could do THAT! I can SIT, for Pete's sake! Any other suggestions for world record feats that I might consider?" --- BOTTOM'S UP IN BOSTON

Dear BOTTOM'S UP: I admire your get-up-and-go, but this may be more than a sitting woman can stand, given your size and admitted lack of fine motor skills. Still, you needn't have Wonder Woman prowess to make or break world records. Examples:

You're writing from Boston, so how about an attempt at eating the most baked beans in the shortest amount of time? Current record is now six pounds in one minute, forty-eight seconds. Or, you just missed this year's Fourth of July Hotdog Eating Contest in Coney Island: Fifty-nine wieners in ten minutes. A tiebreaker had the winner taking the gold in a "Five Dog Eat-Off." Come on, if you can eat one Fenway Frank, you can eat sixty-four. Start training.

Something more unusual? You could attempt to out-undress the Japanese man who can completely strip down in seven seconds flat. Even if you lose, they'll love your attempt on YouTube. Or, the guy who's collected 137 different types of traffic cones (you live in Boston; you could easily best this record by circling one city block).

You may already own a world record, however. You said you were "all thumbs?" The current world record holder has eight, but they're all on one foot. Still, I'd call Guinness.

Thanks for WITBONING, and please keep me posted.

DEAR WITBONES:

"Today I put change in a soda machine and pressed my selection. Nothing came out. I pressed the coin return. Nothing came back. Finally, I tried ALL the buttons, and the one which dropped down was the one brand I wouldn't drink if it was the last fluid on earth. This kind of thing happens to me all the time. I'm always getting robbed by vending machines, of all kinds. What's going on?" --- HELD UP IN HENDERSONVILLE

Dear HELD UP: I went to a gas station this morning for coffee (an inside New England joke) and saw that only the high-test octane was available. All the pumps had their regular and mid-grade pump handles hooded. This is a ruse, of course, because we all know there is only one big tank in the ground.

No one has made a truly high-octane gasoline since the heady Texaco days when five guys in bow ties rushed out and not only fueled your car, but checked your air, oil, windshield wipers and offered to babysit your children.

Soda machine and other related vendors use the same tricky redirection. When not enough of the sugarless, caffeine- and gluten-free tropical citrus root all-organic fruit tea is selling, the machine goes into squelch mode, shutting down the other selections, leaving you with the "last fluid on earth."

Not to worry. You do not have some mysterious, techno-popological, anti-karma thing going on. Machines are not conspiring against you. You're just a victim, along with the rest of us, of unnatural selections.

Thanks for WITBONING, and please keep me posted.

DEAR WITBONES:

"Whatever happened to paper boys (and girls, too)? I miss those neighborhood kids delivering my morning newspaper on their bicycles. Now, it gets mailed to me, and it's always late." --- *NO NEWS IN NORTHFIELD*

Dear NO NEWS: Ah, a touch of nostalgia! Yes, I was one of those speedy deliverers years ago, on my beloved Schwinn Cruiser. Today, you might as well ask whatever happened to chrome forks, steel handlebars, balloon whitewall tires, rubber block pedals, two-tone paint, Phantom grips with multi-colored tassels, fender and rack mounts, and 3-spring padded saddles.

I made enough money as a "paper boy" to keep me in Cherry Bombs, back when those now outlawed ball-shaped firecrackers could blow a hole in your average newspaper (boy) delivery bag.

I'd suggest watching "Leave It To Beaver" reruns until the mail comes.

Thanks for WITBONING, and please keep me posted.

DEAR WITBONES:

"I live in a small Vermont town, and that's my problem. At my age (I'm almost 18), I'm supposed to know what I want to do with my life, but I'm still not sure. Small town or big city? I grew up here, and I feel like I want to stay and go at the same time. Can you help me decide?" --- PERPLEXED IN PEACHAM

Dear PERPLEXED: Ah, sounds like you have the "small town blues," matched in intensity only by its counterpart: the "big city blues." Now, ask yourself what you most gain by staying and least lose by leaving? When you have the answer, ask yourself what you most lose by staying and least gain by leaving. At 18, always feeling like you want to stay and go at the same time is a natural state. You're approaching the (most perplexing) secret of adult life:

We never know the real worthlessness of what we don't have until we gain it, and we never know the real value of what we do have until we lose it. If you've ever lost your car keys or found your brother's scab collection, you know what I mean. Thus, whether or not you remain in Peacham, you'll always know one way of life but never the other.

The answer? Yankee Magazine has designated Peacham, Vermont, as the best village in New England, calling it "unsurpassed." That's reason enough for anyone to remain a lifelong Peachamite.

But, if you have a bad case of surpass and you're not finding your destiny there, I see that you have an historical building in Peacham called: "The Yellow School House." You'll note that today it's painted white.

This is how life works. Not to worry. You'll get there.

Thanks for WITBONING, and please keep me posted.

DEAR WITBONES:

"My wife and I are writing from Rhode Island, and we can tell you that we're sick and tired of being the butt of 'small' jokes. We love our state, we don't FEEL small, and we want all this smalltalk to stop!" --- **BIGGER IN BARRINGTON**

Dear BIGGER: Start here: any non-islandic state with an "island" in its name, already has more built-in grandeur than the rest of us combined, and Rhode Island has more big-ness about it in many other areas. The next time you feel diminished by a "small" joke, fight back with some of these:

You have more doughnut/coffee shops per capita than any other state. That big fact alone has me pondering relocation there. As a humorist, I couldn't muse without my morning java & pastry, so I'd be inspired knowing they're always close by. I've also just learned that coffee milk is Rhode Island's official state drink. Now I'm practically packing my bags.

You're also home to "Nibbles Woodaway," known formerly as "The Big Blue Bug." At 4,000 pounds and 58-feet long, it is easily the world's largest tourist-titillating termite, found on I-95 in Providence (Google it, folks). Take THAT, Texas! Go FISH, Florida!

And, if we're talking proportions, your "Ocean State" has the largest coastline percentage of any state in the U.S., though you'll never get California to admit it.

Rhode Island also has more existing 100-year old homes than the rest of us, easily making you the king of local landmarks, and because of your size, anyone staying in Rhode Island can visit the whole state in the least amount of time. That gives vacationing tourists bigger bangs for their rubbernecking bucks than they'll get anywhere else, and with doughnuts and coffees always right around any corner.

Stand tall! Go big with small!

Thanks for WITBONING, and please keep me posted.

DEAR WITBONES:

"I'd call myself courteous and conscientious when it comes to the road, but I live in Massachusetts, and my job has me traveling extensively in New Hampshire. My license plate obviously informs everyone that I'm a 'Massachusetts driver,' and I'm also a woman. I'm sick of the stereotypes and of all the comments I get, oftentimes with people yelling at me out their windows when I've done nothing wrong. What can I do?" --- NOT A WILD WOMAN IN WEBSTER

Dear NOT A WILD WOMAN: As a New Hampshire native and Granite State motorist, I feel your pain, and I'll try hard to be sympathetic.

I can't speak to the "woman driver" dynamic, at least as it's commonly leveled. I'm male, and I happen to think that women make far better drivers, with one exception. I say this at the risk of advancing other stereotypes, but I can't do anything about what I consider facts.

Women have the capacity for reproduction, which makes you circuitous creatures. This is your one automotive liability, however, because only a woman could be comfortable caught in a rotary, happy to circumnavigate until a solution naturally presents itself, like running out of gas. No man could tolerate a labor & deliverance like that.

Then again, I also have a friend who once couldn't locate her car in a crowded department store parking lot, and she happened upon another woman with the same problem. Together, they teamed up and set off separately, with each finding the other's vehicle. I'd like to see two men do that, or even think about doing it, without crying.

Men may have stamina, but women have endurance. If your average man had to go through childbirth, we'd still all be stuck in jellyfish mode. At the risk of offending half my readership, I believe that, in general, women are just better with all things mechanical.

Right here, I can see my Mr. Fix-It male readers pointing in protest to their garage tool boards as evidence of their mechanical prowess. What folly. As a man in touch with his feminine side, I know that as a wrench, a screwdriver makes a fine hammer, and that pounding a cold steering wheel will jumpstart a dead battery.

My lawnmower will just have to wait for winter.

The Massachusetts driving element of your persecution is another matter, and is always a delicate dilemma. Any "native" of any state naturally feels a kinship with that state's road savvy, and as all of us are natives AND tourists at one time and place or another, the solution lies in giving and taking this problem one driver and one highway at a time.

In New Hampshire, everything is a rotary, and here, if you want to be taken seriously, you should never use your turn signal. It only gives the opposition the illusion of an unfair advantage. We expect you to not signal right and turn left, so you're better off taking us by surprise.

Also, you must forget posted speed limits. The signs are only put there to distract you. Here, there is an unwritten prima facie rule that factors-in local detours, potholes, frost heaves and parades.

Just follow the driver ahead of you. You won't know where he's going, either.

WARNING: You may think that you've found yourself caught in a "parade." You're not. It's the same mistake "Flatlanders" make here when they stop at a yard sale only to discover that it's a family picnic and obsessive-compulsive lawn ornament owners. Just smile and wave.

Remember the old adage: "You can take a woman out of Massachusetts, but you can't make a square rotary." Thus, let's begin the healing by making a general automotive gender-free pact:

If you promise not to give us a honk and harangue for cutting you off in Massachusetts when we realize that we've missed the turn-off to Webster's Lake Chaubunagungamaug, we won't yell at you when you don't signal right, partially turn left, then hit reverse as you discover you're going the wrong way up Bethlehem's Mount Agassiz.

If you can pardon us for losing our way to the biggest lake in Webster, we'll pardon you for backing down a mountain without signaling where you aren't going.

Thanks for WITBONING, and please keep me posted.

DEAR WITBONES:

"I'm fifty years old, and since my fondest desire right now is to live in Florida, where on Earth am I going to retire TO when I turn seventy?" --- WOMAN WONDERING WHERE IN WASHINGTON, D.C.

Dear WOMAN WONDERING: This deserves a longer than usual response, because it sent me reeling into a frenzied research mode, tapping into my favorite and the most fun government agency ever misappropriated: the U.S. Department of Census --- a statistical stewpot of magnificent clutter.

Where else can you sit back and suffer through government gibberish like this:

"Intercensal estimates are different in their interpretation than postcensal estimates, primarily because population change is measured by the difference between two census enumerations, rather than through administrative data on the components of change."

Gulp.

Scary to think about the people who write like that. Scarier to think about the people who THINK like that. Scariest to think about the people who pay attention to it.

But, if we're going to get you to Florida via our nation's capital, we have to make a pit stop at the USDC. It is, after all, the zenith of our tax dollars at play, and it strikes at the heart of your poser. It is the best of what Voltaire called: "the art of government," which he defined as "Taking as much money as possible from one class of citizens to give it to the other."

To be fair, the blame for this doesn't rest entirely with you. I've been watching Court TV all week, and my head is buzzing with legal-speak.

Yesterday, when a particularly pushy cross-examining lawyer challenged the unraveling opposition's witness (as the lawyer pursued what Henry James called: "the fatal futility of fact,"), he was interrupted and admonished by the judge, who told him: "Well, Counselor, if the witness doesn't remember what WAS in that document, chances are she doesn't remember what WASN'T."

Then, your letter arrived, and I was forced to retreat to these frontlines and run amok in wicked sidebars, quoting dead French historians, American novelists, and TV lawyers.

But, we must address your quandary, i.e. where to go once you get where you're going, so here are three fatal but fun futilities culled from my agonizing romp through the USDC's factual databanks. Let's look at these censal side dishes and draw your personal retiree profile and best-case scenario:

1. *"In the year 2030, one in five Americans will be age 65 or older, or approximately 70 million people."*

Thus, wherever you land in 2030, you'll have 70 million peers, myself included, or an approximate 20 percent chance of your being rear-ended by another golf cart driver at the Pensacola Piggly Wiggly and a real albeit remote chance that it will be me.

I don't know the odds of your being clipped by a myopic old humorist cutting through the parking lot on his electric golf trike, and even the USDC makes no reference to this.

You'll recognize me, though. I'll be the duffer lying in a post-catapulted bony heap in your backseat, wearing a day-glo crash helmet with: "WILL PUN FOR SEX" emblazoned in reverse-lettering on the visor.

2. "In 2030, at least 56.5 percent of men over the age of 85 will be married, versus only 15.3 percent of women at that age."

This one must mean that in 2030 the majority of married mid-octogenarian males will either be dead, or married to much younger women, or dead because they married much younger women, OR, they'll be off three-wheeling in supermarket parking lots cruising and crashing into gero-babe buggy bumpers.

3. "The highest percentage of retirees will live in California and Florida. The lowest percentage in Alaska and Wyoming."

Statistically-speaking of the year 2030, it now appears you're at least 25-percent assured of getting your question answered, OR, 75-percent likely to be wondering why you let your philandering Eskimoan husband talk you into buying that Cheyenne condo only to run off with a Sacramento widow, leaving you in a retiring, Sunshine State lurch with an aggravated case of golf cart whiplash and a pun-loving funnyman triker in the back seat.

Hmm. I would appreciate your refraining from putting questions like these to me in the future. I've now been up all night trying to find the demographics on migrating humorists.

And ... winter's coming.

Thanks for WITBONING, and please keep me posted.

DEAR WITBONES:

"I'm 60-years old and attending college for Human Services. Most of the other students are considerably younger than I am. We've had the same instructor for several classes and many of these younger students have become very obnoxious when it comes to listening to him.

"They are whispering very loudly about their weekend plans, their hangovers, or the fact that they are far behind in their final projects. I remind them that other people would like to hear what is being taught, but I am getting really tired of the circus atmosphere, which I am paying big bucks for. The instructor rarely says anything. I have one more year until graduation, and this same group of students will be moving along with me and the same instructor.

"How do I maintain my sanity? --- STUDENT WHISPERER IN WALTHAM.

Dear STUDENT WHISPERER: Congratulations for jumping into a postsecondary pursuit at your age. We're never too old to try new things. We're also never too old to have those things test our sanity.

You don't need a classroom these days to understand why you're surrounded by what I call the "devotees of distraction." You call them "considerably younger" humans, and I've seen a gaggle of them assemble at a café, ignore each other, and begin punching letters into their designer phones and communicating, presumably with another gaggle of modern day telegraphists also busy ignoring each other at another café.

It makes me feel like calling myself up and asking me if I wasn't busy. I didn't, because I wasn't sure I'd answer. I'm also often the last person I want to talk to, but when I do, I like to do it in person.

The key to this, of course, is that "the instructor rarely says anything" to or about your classmates and their untoward behavior. Sounds like he's surrendered to futility, too.

Suggestions: You say they are "whispering very loudly." Another word for this is "talking." You could try talking very loudly. Another word for this is "yelling."

This may shame them into behaving better in class, but I wouldn't count on it. They'll probably just think you're nuts and begin "texting" their friends who are acting out in other classrooms, to tell them all about the yelling old crazy person in theirs.

But, before long, there would be students silently not paying attention in countless schools all across America and you will have saved a generation from itself.

Or, as you cite the "circus atmosphere" that you're finding impossible to endure, you could throw in the Human Resources career towel and run away to clown college, thus turning your life's lemons into a lemonade that might just better serve you and save your sanity.

Thanks for WITBONING, and please keep me posted.

DEAR WITBONES:

"My husband and I are retired New Hampshire natives, and we're spending time over the winter visiting my old college roommate and her family. They're relocated in a southern state so we're really appreciating spending time in a warmer climate. My one complaint is about the food.

She's completely changed the cuisine that we both grew up with in New England and now only prepares and serves "Southern" fare. Wouldn't you think she'd think to make meals that we were all familiar and comfortable with rather than these strange (and frankly, hard to digest) dishes? How can I gently suggest this to her before our next visit?" --- *NO APPETITE IN NEW ORLEANS*

Dear NO APPETITE: As a fellow Granite Stater, I've got to stop you right there and "gently suggest" that you pack up your appetite, your attitude, and go home. If your old friend had wanted her life to remain "familiar and comfortable," she wouldn't have given up corn chowda and Yankee Doodle noodles for jambalaya and crawfish pie.

You're her guests. And, you're living on the cheap in nice weather while I'm back here chipping the ice off my windshield with an overdrawn debit card. My advice? Be gracious, be grateful, quit whining and learn to love gumbo.

Thanks for WITBONING, and please keep me posted.

DEAR WITBONES:

"I am about to be a remarried woman heading into my late middle-aged years. When I tell my friends and colleagues that they'll need to update their address books and email files with my new last name after my wedding, I am frequently asked (and rather aggressively, too), 'Why will you change your name?! You don't have to do that, you know!' It's really beginning to bother me. I have a hard time explaining it, and I'm tired of trying. Can you help me with a response?" --- NOM DE GROOM IN GRAFTON

Dear NOM DE GROOM: History is full of research on this subject, and your problem prompted me to look at some of it, discovering what is and has been lawful & traditional through the centuries and around the world.

Well, I'm not going to get into any of that. You can Google "maiden name" and get the same 29,100,000 results that I did. You're clearly here looking for some quick and practical retorts for your cronies, and you're in luck, because I too am "heading into my late middle-aged years" and last year I remarried.

Before we wed, I non-aggressively asked Diane Lillian Church if she was planning to change her name. I told her I was okay with whatever she decided. She said that she wanted to be Mrs. Sherman.

When I asked her why (again, without a hint of aggression), she said "because I want to be."

Now, I didn't get this far in life without knowing when to stop priming the pump, so I let it be right there. But, I sense that this is the same response you've been giving your friends and colleagues, and it's leaving you peeved and them unsatisfied.

I'd be remiss in my agony uncle duty if I didn't let you know that you do have other options besides a complete birth name surrender and a new designation. You could use your maiden name as your new middle name. Or, in nine states, your spouse could change his last name to yours. Or (my favorite) you could legally "blend" your names.

If Diane and I had wanted, we could now be the Churchmans or the Shmurches, or we could've even anagrammed Church/Sherman and re-dubbed ourselves: Mr. & Mrs. Hunchcharmers. We actually did discuss doing the latter, as a way to create exactly the kind of thing that you're trying to avoid. A little public and private spectacle on occasion is good for the soul:

"Hunchcharmers? Party of two?" What fun.

Now, what to say to anyone who demands to know why you're electing to drop your surname? How should you respond when they tell you that you don't have to do that? Hmmm ....

When I'm out on the Harley pulled over somewhere, and someone inevitably make my business their business and asks me why I'm not wearing a helmet, I stare at them with as much mock shock as I can muster, and say, "Oh ... you mean ... they make HELMETS?? What a great idea!"

Try a variation of this with your contacts.

Thanks for WITBONING, and please keep me posted.

DEAR WITBONES:

"I am an old man. How old? Here's how old: Something is happening to me now that started some time ago as an occasional thing, but now it goes on all the time. People talk to me like I'm hard of hearing or senile, shouting at me and/or speaking very slowly. What can I do about it? It makes me mad and depressed. What can I say to these people without offending them?" --- **NOT DUMB OR DEAF IN DANVILLE**

Dear NOT DUMB OR DEAF: Let's start at the end of your letter, and begin with you not worrying about offending anyone who begins their conversation by offending you. They're in need of a comeuppance. Instead, it's time for you to have some fun with this.

In defense of people (always a hard thing for me to do, but I try), they mean well most of the time. For instance, people often turn to me for help because I'm a writer, so they believe that I must know the difference, e.g., between an assumption and a presumption.

Turns out I do, but I try not to lord it over anyone. I could *assume*, for example, based on the scant evidence you've provided, that you look and act like a rickety-pickety, crotchety old wretch of a man who mostly ignores everyone, drives for miles with his turn signal on, makes awful noises when he eats, wears mismatched socks and talks to himself in public, but I shouldn't *presume* that.

It's clear, however, that you have become a victim of the all-too-common discrimination of ageism. I can safely presume that.

But, before you go much further, you should make sure that you're NOT hard of hearing. People may be yelling at you because you're not otherwise reacting to them. How else would you know? Go get your hearing checked. I'll wait.

Now, all okay? CAN...YOU...HEAR...ME? PUT YOUR GLASSES ON!

(Sorry, I couldn't resist, but as an advancing upper middle-ager, I'm simpatico and entitled.)

I did mean what I said up there, though. You do need to give up the anger and despair, and instead turn this into a source of entertainment for you. Have fun. BE fun.

Next time you're spoken to like you're ... well ... as you say: dumb and deaf, try this:

<u>Stranger:</u> "EX...CUSE...ME, SIR. ARE...YOU...LOST?"

<u>You:</u> "No, I'm tense, but it's okay. I've been in the past, tense; I'm now in the present, tense, but once you go screw yourself, I won't be in the future, tense."

Think about this for a while, and come up with your own list of snappy retorts.

You could also take the initiative on occasion, and speak softly to a stranger, whispering something, anything. It doesn't matter. Most people now, as you yourself painfully report, increasingly think you're damaged goods, anyway.

When they apologize (and they will) for not being able to understand you, simply yell: "WHAT ARE YOU ... DUMB AND DEAF?"

Thanks for WITBONING, and please keep me posted.

DEAR WITBONES:

"Recently, I treated a young friend to lunch at a special, very expensive restaurant to celebrate the successful end of her school term. Our food looked delicious when it arrived, but one of the almonds in my baby spinach salad was too hard to chew and turned out to be a false fingernail! I tucked it into my napkin and didn't mention it to anyone as I didn't want to ruin the festive occasion.

My problem now is that she's written to ask if she can take ME to dinner after her graduation ... at this same restaurant! I don't want to tell her what happened there, but I can't bring myself to go back. What should I do?" --- **FINGER FOODS IN FREEPORT**

Dear FINGER FOODS: First, congratulations to you for not making a scene at the time, but had you acted reflexively by shrieking "HEY! What's this freakin' fake fingernail doing in my spinach?!" ... none of us would have blamed you.

Indeed, it must have taken all your composure to finish the meal without letting on or showing your disgust. I'd like to know how you got through an entree & dessert without imagining all kinds of suspect culinary intruders. Was that an eyelash in your vitello tonnato? Could that extra crunch in your chocolate chestnut cake have been a stud earring?

Try not to think about it.

Yes, obviously, you can't return there. Your friend wouldn't understand why you're scrutinizing every dish like a mad scientist and demanding an up-close inspection of all ten fingers and both ears & eyes of your server. But, you will need a good reason to redirect both of you to an alternate eatery.

Try this:

Tell her that you've developed deipnophobia --- a rare but very real abnormal fear of dinner conversation --- and that you wouldn't want to ruin your meal together by being mute.

Thanks for WITBONING, and please keep me posted.

DEAR WITBONES:

"I am a real animal lover so I offered to care for my friend's large elderly dog and housesit at her home while she was vacationing for a week. The dog had always been friendly and seemed to enjoy my earlier visits, but he repeatedly snarled at me when the family was away and I was alone with him. I stayed in the house with the dog just one night, slept in my car one night, then gave up and drove back and forth between my parents' home and hers the other days to check in on the dog and leave food and water. Still, I'm afraid my friend will never trust me again if I tell her what happened. What should I do?" --- DOG-DAZED IN DARIEN

Dear DOG-DAZED: Let's look at the psychology of this, assuming the dog survived your care.

You say that the dog was always friendly with you and seemed to enjoy your earlier visits when your friend was present, but when you were alone with the dog, it turned on you. I believe we're at the crux of the biscuit.

Does this happen in your personal and/or professional relationships with people? We're always quick to blame a dog's misbehaviors on the dog, when in fact the dog is only reacting to something we did or didn't do.

Did you bring the proper chew-toys and treats? You mentioned that it was an old big dog. Did you think to bring his Classic Milk-Bones, or did you just thoughtlessly grab whatever was on the shelf, and walk in with small-dog Pup-eroni snacks or toy dog Jumbones? Did you remember to set the TV to the Animal Channel? Did you move his blank-y?

As for telling your friend, best leave sleeping lies to the dog.

Thanks for WITBONING, and please keep me posted.

DEAR WITBONES:

"I've just read a news story on the subject of cow-tipping. A university zoology professor in Canada says that two people could tip over a cow in theory, but only if the cow has a 'rigid, unresponding body,' which it doesn't. Can you settle this?" --- LEANING IN LAKE CHARLES

Dear LEANING: First, I'd like to know why Canadian taxpayers are paying a university professor to research the finer points of bovine balance. I was about to investigate this when, speaking of wastes and excesses, I saw where American taxpayers have been billed $50,000 to promote the Annual Hawaii Chocolate Festival.

You could've tipped me over with a lei of Hershey's Kisses.

But, just for you, I've checked with my scientist wife (an expert on the subject of dealing with a sometimes stiff, sometimes unresponsive mate), and she assures me that the Canadian prof is correct, if it's true that said cows were paralyzed with either fright or mating stimuli.

We'll leave the theorists to determine the best ways to either terrify or titillate a cow.

Thanks for WITBONING, and please keep me posted.

DEAR WITBONES:

"Did you see the story on fat cats? University scientists here are saying that calico cat chromosome studies may help show why some humans have problems with obesity. What gives with that? I'm not fat, but I do have a few extra pounds." --- CORPULENT CALICO KITTY IN CLOVERDALE

Dear CORPULENT CALICO KITTY: Yes, I did see that article, and I think I can help.

Calico cats are almost always female, which means they have two X chromosomes. Male cats have an X and a Y chromosome. The same goes for humans, minus the hairballs.

As you know from your high school math and science classes, whenever you have a known value of X and an unknown value of Y in an equation, you must use Pi to find the answer.

Logic then tells us that calico cats, often along with their human owners, are probably fatter because they eat more Pi.

Thanks for WITBONING, and please keep me posted.

DEAR WITBONES:

"I saw a wildlife show on TV where it showed that alligators are now climbing trees, but as if this isn't scary enough, it also had a report on toads out there with 'weaponized mustaches.' What the heck is going on with Mother Nature?" --- **FREAKED OUT IN FLAGLER BEACH**

Dear FREAKED OUT: Yes, unfortunately for you, it's true that alligators are now climbing trees, but according to scientists at the University of Tennessee, "only as long as footholds are available." You may thus conclude that it's scary to live in Florida and easy to be a scientist in Tennessee.

And, yes, there are male frogs in a remote mountainous region of China that are equipped with "spines on their upper lips," which are used to combat other male toads while guarding their nests.

Canadian scientist Cameron Hudson warns us, however, that "they do try to stab you a bit if you try to pick them up." Now you know that it's also easy to be a scientist in Canada studying horny-lipped toads in China.

I haven't conducted a scientific study, but I think that the mustachicles I sported through this past sub-zero winter could've easily out-stabbed any Chinese rival.

Thanks for WITBONING, and please keep me posted.

DEAR WITBONES:

"Why is my image reversed when I look into a mirror? Does this make sense to you?" --- *LOOKING BACK IN LEWISBURG*

Dear LOOKING BACK: Science tells us that mirrors work when photons cause our atomic electrons to vibrate.

Thus, "If I was a mirror, you'd be vibrating all over, baby," is a great inside pickup line for atomic scientists.

Let's leave it there.

Thanks for WITBONING, and please keep me posted.

DEAR WITBONES:

"I'm what you might call a nature lover, and I enjoy back yard sunbathing in my altogether. Trouble is, I'm now a victim of 21st Century technology, because lately I've seen those little drones flying around when I'm naked out there. Should I worry that one of these days I'm going to be famous on YouTube for the wrong reason? How can I protect myself from these prying eyes in the sky? What can I do to keep my life (and my airspace!) private?" --- BARE IN SANTA BARBARA

Dear BARE: As a Californian, you'll be encouraged to know that your Governor has signed a bill prohibiting photographers from using drones to photograph celebrities on private properties at an altitude below 350 feet. It was designed to keep those prying eyes you cite from becoming high-tech Peeping Tom paparazzi profiteers. Thus, your first line of defense is to avoid ever becoming a celebrity and to remain at sea level.

But, it not easy to not become a celebrity. These days, it's so easy to become famous, we have to work at remaining anonymous (or in your case, just another naked Golden Stater).

Today, there's almost no privacy no matter where we go, clothed or in the buff. By the end of any average day in public, we've all been videoed at least half a dozen times --- at banks, department stores, town halls, fast-food drive-thrus, hospitals, health clubs --- and let's not forget Google Maps.

Because you sent me your street address, I can follow along in street view, and see where you live. Yep, there's your home. Hey, nice porch, cool wind chimes, but I'm not a big fan of pink flamingo lawn ornaments. Now, let's see, if I switch to satellite view, I can see ... YIKES!

Right about here, I'd suggest a backyard beach umbrella.

Thanks for WITBONING, and please keep me posted.

DEAR WITBONES:

"Here we are again, rockin' around the 'holiday' versus 'Christmas' politically correct tree, and I've about had enough of this nonsense. If I say 'Merry Christmas,' I'm being insensitive to non-Christians, but if I say 'Happy Holidays,' I feel like I'm being denied my religious freedom. What can I do to keep everyone happy, beginning with me? And, please, no Jesus jokes about my home town." --- CONFUSED IN CORPUS CHRISTI

Dear CONFUSED: A long time ago, when I began writing humor as means of insuring a substandard living wage, I swore to never write about religion or politics. Both have now morphed into what the Urban Dictionary calls "Religitics," so I've given up on that oath.

I'd never make jokes about your home town. Its name translates from the Latin as "Body of Christ," but you'll have to sort that out for yourself. I write from Bethlehem, NH, so I'm really not one to talk. People travel to our post office from far and away at Christmas just to get this little town's postmark on their holiday cards and packages. Well, one person's Holy validation is another's non-fragile, non-liquid, non-hazardous, non-perishable priority mail, I always say.

Yesterday, I was speaking with a cashier in the checkout line at a department store. In the true spirit of remaining seasonably religitical, I will not name either of them here. When she handed me my Tums and eggnog, she blurted out "Merry Christmas," but quickly corrected herself: "Oh, I'm sorry, I'm not supposed to say that," she apologized.

"Not to worry," I said. "I forgive you."

I think Jesus would've given me an attaboy.

Funny you should mention rockin' around the tree, prompting this seriocomic historical footnote: let's not forget that Christmas trees in this country were once deemed symbols of "pagan mockery and heathen traditions" by our Puritan forebears, and because I'm a big fan of history (after all, it's the birthplace of some of our best facts), I hold with H.L. Mencken's definition of a Puritan, which still rings true today as the model for too many blowhard holdouts from the good ol' 17th Century: "A Puritan is one who suspects somewhere someone is having a good time."

My Grandma had a great leveler for anyone caught in your moral dilemma. She'd tell you: "Whatever flips your skirt."

So, why not, whatever your madcap persuasion, if someone wishes you a Merry Christmas, just thank them, give it right back and Merrily move on? If they hope you have a Happy Holiday, let your secular light shine and fire off your best Happy Ditto in their direction. No different if you get hit with a Kwanzaa, or a Hanukkah, or even a Pancha Ganapati:

"Hey, I appreciate it, and same to you, buddy!"

Now, what should YOU say this time of year, if you find yourself greeting someone first and you want to wish them well? Best to just go with "How about those Red Sox?"

Trust me, this will even work in Texas, generating some good will and world peace before you part company.

Thanks for WITBONING, and please keep me posted.

DEAR WITBONES:

"I was going to write to 'Dear Abby' with my problem, but your name came up at a cocktail party by someone who swore that you helped her AND made her laugh. Right now I could use some of both, and here's why: my boyfriend has just told me that he's gay. I thought something was up because of how he'd been treating me lately (and NOT treating me) in bed. Now, is this my fault? I've always been there for him, in every way. What didn't I do? What should I do now??? --- SEXLESS IN SWANSBORO

Dear SEXLESS: First, I'm flattered (and a tad nervous) that I was the chit-chat subject at a party where people assemble to drink and test-drive their epitaphs, but you didn't mention what I allegedly did to help and amuse your friend. (Was she from Telluride? Did she have red hair and an old Volvo? Never mind.)

Next, your boyfriend's sexual orientation is what it is because of who he is and what he does, not because of who you are and what you don't do. Let me try that again: He isn't what he isn't because of who he isn't and what he doesn't do, not because of who you aren't and what you do do.

Get it? He's not straight. You are.

Still confused? Okay ... let's use food to answer this:

I don't like Lima beans. I've never liked Lima beans. I don't know why, and I've never worried about it.

I do, however, like peas. In fact, I love peas. I've always loved peas. I don't know why, and I've never worried about it.

It's just the way I've always lived with legumes, because most legumes are vegetables, but not all vegetables are legumes. You might start by living like food.

Thanks for WITBONING, and please keep me posted.

    B. Elwin Sherman lives in the New England north country with his wife Diane. He is an author, poet, humor columnist and agony uncle.

    He is a dog person, but she has two cats.

    She is a power walker, but he takes the bus.

    Every day, they look more and more like their caricatures.

    Love is the perfection of differences.

www.ingramcontent.com/pod-product-compliance
Lightning Source LLC
Chambersburg PA
CBHW020013050426
42450CB00005B/453